THE WORLD OF OCEAN ANIMALS
HARP SEALS

by Mari Schuh

pogo

Ideas for Parents and Teachers

Pogo Books let children practice reading informational text while introducing them to nonfiction features such as headings, labels, sidebars, maps, and diagrams, as well as a table of contents, glossary, and index.

Carefully leveled text with a strong photo match offers early fluent readers the support they need to succeed.

Before Reading

• "Walk" through the book and point out the various nonfiction features. Ask the student what purpose each feature serves.

• Look at the glossary together. Read and discuss the words.

Read the Book

• Have the child read the book independently.

• Invite him or her to list questions that arise from reading.

After Reading

• Discuss the child's questions. Talk about how he or she might find answers to those questions.

• Prompt the child to think more. Ask: Harp seals swim in icy ocean waters. What other animals swim in icy waters?

Pogo Books are published by Jump!
5357 Penn Avenue South
Minneapolis, MN 55419
www.jumplibrary.com

Library of Congress Cataloging-in-Publication Data

Names: Schuh, Mari C., 1975- author.
Title: Harp seals / by Mari Schuh.
Description: Minneapolis: Jump!, Inc., [2022]
Series: The world of ocean animals
Includes index. | Audience: Ages 7-10
Identifiers: LCCN 2020050877 (print)
LCCN 2020050878 (ebook)
ISBN 9781636900544 (hardcover)
ISBN 9781636900551 (paperback)
ISBN 9781636900568 (ebook)
Subjects: LCSH: Harp seal–Juvenile literature.
Classification: LCC QL737.P64 S38 2022 (print)
LCC QL737.P64 (ebook) | DDC 599.79/29–dc23
LC record available at https://lccn.loc.gov/2020050877
LC ebook record available at https://lccn.loc.gov/2020050878

Editor: Jenna Gleisner
Designer: Michelle Sonnek

Photo Credits: Dolores M. Harvey/Shutterstock, cover, 8-9; All Canada Photos/Alamy, 1, 5, 6-7; COULANGES/Shutterstock, 3, 18-19; Hatt Photography/Shutterstock, 4; MB Photography/Getty, 10-11; Tory Kallman/Shutterstock, 12; Paul Souders/Getty, 13; Michio Hoshino/Minden Pictures/SuperStock, 14-15; slowmotiongli/Shutterstock, 16; slowmotiongli/iStock, 17, 23; Joe BUNNI/Getty, 20-21.

Printed in the United States of America at Corporate Graphics in North Mankato, Minnesota.

TABLE OF CONTENTS

CHAPTER 1

· ·

A COLD,
ICY HOME

A harp seal rests on the ice.
It is tired from swimming and
hunting in the cold ocean.

Adult harp seals are gray. Their faces are black. Each seal has a black marking on its back. Adults are about five to six feet (1.5 to 1.8 meters) long. They can weigh up to 300 pounds (136 kilograms).

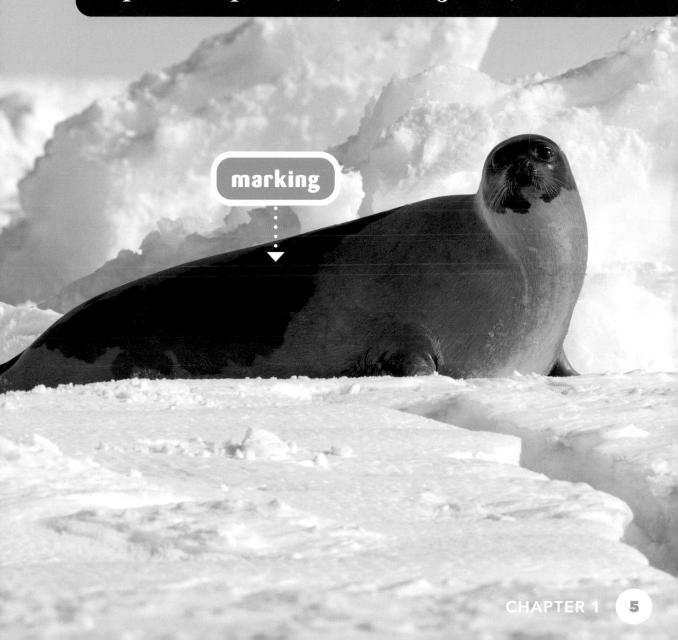

marking

Blubber keeps harp seals warm. Their short fur **repels** water. Strong flippers help them swim. Whiskers **sense** movement in the water. They help seals find **prey**.

TAKE A LOOK!

What are a harp seal's body parts called? Take a look!

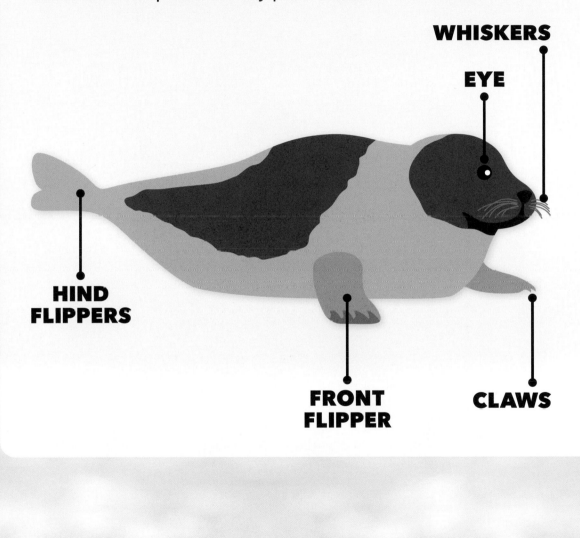

WHISKERS

EYE

HIND FLIPPERS

FRONT FLIPPER

CLAWS

Harps seals live in the Arctic and North Atlantic Oceans. They spend most of their time in the icy water.

TAKE A LOOK!

Where do harp seals live? Take a look!

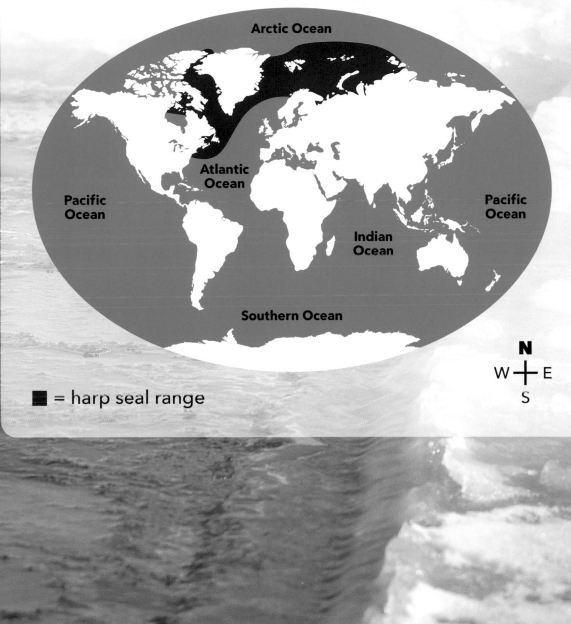

Arctic Ocean

Atlantic
Ocean

Pacific
Ocean

Pacific
Ocean

Indian
Ocean

Southern Ocean

■ = harp seal range

N
W ⊕ E
S

Harp seals dive and swim. They **migrate** north in the summer. There, they hunt and eat. They travel south again for the winter to **mate**.

CHAPTER 2

SURVIVING IN THE OCEAN

Polar bears, orcas, and large sharks are **predators**. They hunt harp seals. But harp seals are fast swimmers. They can swim away. They can also go onto land to get away.

orca

Harp seals hunt small fish and **crustaceans**. They eat many kinds.

capelin fish

Harp seals dive to find prey. They can stay underwater for 15 minutes! They come to the surface to breathe.

Harp seals have **flexible** bodies. They twist and turn as they hunt. They have long jaws and many teeth. These help harp seals catch prey.

CHAPTER 3

PUPS AND COLONIES

Harp seals are **mammals**. Each year, a mother gives birth to just one **pup**. She does this on the ice. The pup stays on the ice. It drinks its mother's milk. Mothers feed their pups for about 12 days. As the pups grow, their bodies make blubber.

pup

Females gather in big **colonies**. Several thousand might be on the ice. The crowd is huge! So how does a female find her pup? Each mother knows its pup by its smell.

Fluffy white fur covers the pups. The thick fur keeps them warm. The white color blends in with snow and ice. This helps keep pups safe from predators.

DID YOU KNOW?

Pups **molt** many times. Older seals molt every spring. They grow a new coat of fur.

After many weeks, the young seals go into the water. They swim and find food on their own. They learn to live in the cold ocean.

DID YOU KNOW?

Hunting, **pollution**, oil spills, and fishing nets harm harp seals. Melting ice from **climate change** also affects them. They need ice for their young and for protection. How can you help keep harp seals safe?

ACTIVITIES & TOOLS

MAKE BLUBBER GLOVES

In this experiment, learn how blubber keeps seals warm in cold, icy water.

What You Need:
- a large bowl or bucket
- ice cubes
- water
- two plastic food storage bags
- shortening
- duct tape
- towels or paper towels for cleaning up

❶ Fill a large bowl or bucket with ice and water.

❷ Fill one plastic bag with shortening.

❸ Put one hand in an empty plastic bag. Put the other hand in the bag filled with shortening.

❹ Have an adult carefully tape the bags closed around your wrists to keep out water.

❺ Move the shortening around so that it completely covers your hand.

❻ Now put both hands in the ice water. What do you notice? How does the shortening work like blubber?

blubber: A thick layer of fat under the skin of some ocean animals.

climate change: Changes in Earth's weather and climate over time.

colonies: Groups of harp seals.

crustaceans: Types of ocean animals that have outer skeletons, such as lobsters, crabs, and shrimp.

flexible: Able to bend or move easily.

mammals: Warm-blooded animals that give birth to live young, which drink milk from their mothers.

mate: To join together to produce young.

migrate: To travel from one place to another place during different times of the year.

molt: To lose old fur, feathers, or skin so that new layers can grow.

pollution: Harmful materials that damage or contaminate the air, water, or soil.

predators: Animals that hunt other animals for food.

prey: Animals that are hunted by other animals for food.

pup: A young harp seal.

repels: Keeps away.

sense: To feel or become aware of something.

INDEX

TO LEARN MORE

Finding more information is as easy as 1, 2, 3.

❶ Go to www.factsurfer.com

❷ Enter "harpseals" into the search box.

❸ Choose your book to see a list of websites.

FACT SURFER